THIS IS MY OFFERING

First published in 2018 by
New Life Publishing,
Bedfordshire LU4 9HG

British Library Cataloguing in Publication Data
A catalogue record for this book is available
from the British Library

ISBN   978 1 912237 05 0

Unless otherwise stated, Bible references are
from the New International Version © 1973,
The International Bible Society,
and are used with permission.

Typesetting by New Life Publishing,
Luton, UK www.goodnewsbooks.co.uk
Printed and bound in Great Britain

This is My Offering

Bob Light

WHAT'S YOUR STORY
The Complete
Self-publishing Service

Dedication

For my loving wife, Colette,
and my three children
Zoë, Jessica, and Sam.

'This is my offering, dear Lord
this is my offering to you, God
I will give you my life
for it's all I have to give
because you gave your life for me
I stand before you at this altar
so many have given you more
I may not have much I can offer
Yet what I have is truly yours
This is my offering
This is my offering, dear Lord'

(Third Day)

Contents

Foreword

When Bob asked me if I would consider writing the foreword for his new book, I jumped at the opportunity! I first met Bob and Colette on a church Missions Trip to the UK over twenty years ago. It was there that I met a couple who gave from their hearts all that they had to the poor and needy, the sick, those who were down and out, the widows and orphans and those in prison. I have seen Bob literally give someone in a desperate place, the coat off his back! This gives me the opportunity to introduce you to one of the most incredible couples that I have ever met.

The way I typically describe Bob is 'Mother Teresa in a sixty-something reformed heroin addict's body'. Together they are like the Duracell Bunny – they keep going and going and giving and giving, with all that is in them. They are the epitome of what real Christians look like.

As you read this book, you will find story after story of how God has touched the lives of people through their Ministry and you can't help but be moved with compassion. You will see God's people, those who are struggling, through the eyes of the Father. You will see them as Bob and Colette see them. Hopefully you will be inspired in some way to want to help and love those in need. If God can use Bob, a heroin addict for over 27 years, He can use you! There is no person on this planet God does not have a good plan and purpose for.

My prayer is that God will touch your heart through reading this book and you will be able to grasp how wide and long and high and deep God's love is for you and all His children. That you will be able to experience His love which goes beyond all knowledge, so that you will be filled to the measure of all the fullness of God; that your lives would become living stories of God's goodness, just as Bob and Colette's lives are, to be used to give glory to God.

Just a side note, in all my years of knowing Bob, he has never asked for a penny to help his Ministry. He and his wife live on nothing, but give all that they have away. He would never ask, but I am asking for him if you would consider donating to their Ministry? Thank you and God Bless you!

Gary Stache
(Best Friend and supporter of Flower of Justice Ministry - California, USA)

I t is truly no coincidence that Bob is called Light. He was born to do just that! Bring light, hope and love into the lives of countless hundreds of needy, often desperate families, particularly on the housing estate where Bob himself was born.

Bob's testimony recounts his journey to HELL and back that his habit had taken him on. It was at that stage – 'the coming back' that I met him. There were however a lot of 'pieces' that needed picking up!

Words cannot fully express the sheer joy of leading a sinner in true repentance through the encounter with Christ into salvation. So too is the amazing experience of being involved and seeing a tormented soul being set free and delivered from Satan's hold and the controlling demons that have lodged there. Of such, Bob needs no reminder!

Bob's introduction to our lives I count as yet one more divine privileged appointment. I was present at the meeting where he got gloriously saved and it was at that point that the Lord most surely entwined our lives.

Hilda and I regularly recall the many times Bob discovered how real the Holy Bible is when we gathered around the large dining room table… he almost devoured the Word of God! It reminded me of the excitement of the children on Christmas morning on opening their presents. The Bible as we know is a LIVING WORD and it was often the case as if the HOLY SPIRIT would suddenly reveal a truth to us causing it to almost jump off the page!

Oh the joy of it! Bob always kept a journal (which I am sure he still has) of all that was promised to him in the Scriptures. I know they became like a life blood stream to him.

I leave my esteemed brother in the Lord to tell his amazing story but one highlight of his life for me has to be the night in the dining room of our farmhouse at Melorne. Our visiting speaker was David Chaudhary – itinerant preacher – full of the Holy Spirit – and who had earlier led Bob to Christ. David prayed for Bob and we witnessed Jesus set him miraculously free from being a lifelong chain tobacco smoker – never to return to the addiction again.

Ours is the God of 'the how much more', so added as it were to his miracles, the Lord brought him the most assuredly amazing Colette and her lovely young daughter, Zoë. The ministry they share together – Zoë now following her career in London – has God's fingerprints all over it! You have shown people the richness of God's kingdom through your sacrificial giving of yourselves in an area where the needs are limitless.

It is God's doing that we met and our privilege to have been one small cog in this ministry wheel of LOVE, JOY and GRACE you have set in motion.

Thanks for such an INIMITABLE friendship. Hilda and I with the whole family, plus Church are greatly honoured and humbled by your God given and Christ-like example.

Ken and Hilda Macleod
(Pastors and dear friends - Camelford, Cornwall)

Introduction

This is a simple book, written to show you the power of God who is able to transform your life and your mind, if you choose to let Him. I pray this book will encourage you to discover a real relationship with the Holy Spirit and that you will know His presence with you.

Each chapter is divided into two parts: my old life and my new life with Jesus. In the redemption stories (my new life) I have tried to show you how God redeems even the negative things that have happened in your life, and turns them around to be used for His good. He even takes you back to places where you were a mess and uses your experience to help others have the hope that things can change. In other words, He takes you back where you were in defeat and leads you into victory. What an amazing saviour! People who looked down on you, now ask you for help and advice.

Jesus took me back to the area where I was in a mess and showed everyone what He can do through one life. 'This is my offering' to the one who saved me: Jesus!

Prologue

I was born in Southampton in 1951, the second of four siblings. My parents and older brother Barry lived in a one bed place, but soon after I was born, we moved to Mayfield Road, as we were entitled to a Council house. My mum had grown up there and my dad had family living on the Flowers' Estate nearby[1]. Three years later we were joined by my sister, Sue. Then another three years later my youngest brother Steve was born. Despite there being four of us, we were the smallest family in our street. Most families had eight or more children!

I had plenty of other relatives living nearby too. My grandad lived on a street called Lilac Road. He had left school at 14 to work in a local mill, grinding flour and working in the bakery. After this, he worked in Loman's Bakery, which was one of the biggest bakeries in town. He worked there his whole life.

His wife, my Nan, was the only Christian in our family and she went to a church in town called Above Bar. She used to walk miles every Sunday to attend. My other Nan lived on our road and I had aunts and uncles living in the streets nearby. I also had cousins living all over the city. My extended family was big!

---

[1] The Flowers' Estate (or Flower Roads) consists of affordable housing built by local government to support low income families.

We were just like all the other working class families in our street. My Dad worked for Shipping Contractors at Southampton Docks and my mum stayed at home with us kids. The docks were a big part of my life, as most of the men in our family worked there. I had a few temporary jobs there myself.

We lived in a three bed house. I shared a bedroom with both my brothers and dreamed of having my own room one day. We were poor, but we lived well - We always had plenty of fruit and veg. As well as his job, my dad was also on the fiddle;[2] everyone round our way was!

At the front of our house, we had an allotment where my uncle grew veg. He was always giving us rhubarb and stuff like that and our neighbours kept chickens. People were much more self-sufficient in those days and we shared with each other. Wherever we went, people knew us, so us kids could play outside and feel safe. We just used to hang around together and play in the street.

I have fond memories of going to Saturday flicks[3] at ABC Minors, as a child. My Uncle worked there as a cinematographer and my Aunty was an Usherette. All the kids in our street used to go together and for the next week would be acting out the movies we'd seen. When we got older, we'd pay for the cheap seats then bundle our way to the pricier top rows. There were so many of us, the staff couldn't stop us!

Also, my dad used to take us down to Mudeford, and we'd enjoy a day on the beach. We thought it was like going abroad. We'd

[2] Engaged in cheating or swindling
[3] Cinema

play in the sand and sometimes swim – we all had to learn to swim at school, in those days. For us, a day in Mudeford was our holiday!

My parents were good parents. My dad was a bit hard; he was screwed up by the war. He had shell shock and used to get really angry, but he brought us up to be polite and we were happy.

Every Sunday they sent us kids down the road to Sunday School, then we'd get dressed up and head to my Nan's for Sunday lunch. We had treats like jelly and I'd play cards with my granddad. My grandparents were always really kind to me, even when I was at my worst.

I used to spend a lot of time with my Nan on my mum's side too. She lived near some woods and would teach me about all the different birds. She understood the seasons, so would take me out foraging and blackberry picking. We could spend all day in the woods by her house. You could walk for miles before they built the M27! She never judged me or put me down and always had time for me.

I enjoyed school as a young child too. I went to Swaythling Primary and it was a lovely little place. They really looked after us. We were all given free school meals and free milk every day, plus vitamins thanks to the new welfare state.

All the dinner ladies were local mums, so we knew if we didn't eat our vegetables, we wouldn't get our pudding! When we got home, we'd have bread and jam for tea or sometimes my mum would get out a pot of dripping for us to dip bread into.

Things changed for me when I went to senior school. In 1963 I was sent to Glen Eyre, the local boys' school and from day one I had to fight my way through it. I was put on a technical course and for the first three years did technical drawing, training to be a draftsman. After 3 years, it was decided my stream would be a grammar stream, so I did English, Art and Geography.

As I got older, other boys would want to fight me, so I started getting into bother. I didn't really like fighting, but I could look after myself. Most days I would walk home and there'd be someone in the cut way waiting to jump me.

I started getting in trouble with the police too. I remember I was sent to court one day for poaching and the judge was my headmaster! He wasn't allowed to hear my case because he knew me, but he said "I'll see you outside my office in the morning!"

There was a lot of crime on our estate, but to us it was normal because we grew up with it. It's only when people look at it from the outside that they think it is bad. You just sort of get used to it all. The Flowers' Estate had a bad reputation, but it was just like most poor areas. Fights and theft weren't unusual to us!

I was really into the music scene in the 1960s. I loved the Kinks, The Stones and other bands. They were all heavily into the drug scene at the time. My dad would get us tickets for gigs, then we'd open a fire exit for all our mates to get in! I've always loved music.

I was passionate about politics at the time too. I was part of AAP, the Association Against Apartheid happening in South Africa and I'd protest about the Vietnam War. I couldn't bear to see injustice in the world. I got caught up in it all really. Stuff like that really upset me, even as a young teenager. I didn't realise at the time, that this desire for justice was something Jesus had put inside me. All of these factors: the environment I lived in, the music scene and the crazy world around me, led to me making some very poor decisions. But little did I know, God had a plan...

Addiction

'Since your love got hold of me,
I'm a new creation, I'm forever changed'
(*United Pursuit- 'Since Your Love'*)

I started taking drugs when I was 12. Mainly cannabis, but I started doing a bit of acid and tried opium once or twice. It was the 1960s and things were changing for young people. Drugs were appearing on the scene, but at that time it was just me and one other guy on the Flowers' Estate doing them; no one really understood it or knew much about it. We both became heroin addicts in the end…

When I was 15 I tried to buy some cannabis down town, but it was a bit of a dry time. So I bought some off this guy I met and we started hanging out in the parks, smoking dope together.

Then he offered me some little white tablets. Turns out they were diamorphine hydrochloride: Heroin, or smack as we called it. I told him I didn't like needles and I wasn't going to start injecting myself with anything, I didn't even like the jabs at school! He kept on at me to try it and as we were stoned I said, 'Yeah go on then, just do it.' The first hit was free, but I paid for it after that.

That was it really. In my mind I had found something that shut everything out. I was fed up of the world around me. I'd had enough of seeing images of the Vietnam War and all the injustices in the world. I couldn't change anything, so this was a way to block it all out.

The next day I was down at the chemist scoring 60mg of pharmaceutical heroin off the other addicts for £1. It was only the size of a coffee sweetener, but it was powerful stuff.

I went every morning after that to score[1] , then I'd go to school. From that age on I was addicted... I even sat my GCEs whilst on heroin! A few times, the teachers found me crashed out in the toilet, but they just thought I was stressed because of the exams. By the time I left school that May, I went straight to the GP, showed him the track marks on my arms and he prescribed me heroin.

There were five other addicts in the city at that time and I was number 367 in the whole country. I had a yellow prescription, different from the ordinary white ones, marking me out as a registered addict. The first time I showed up to collect my script, our local chemist said, 'I've been dreading this day.' They used to open up early for us, as they didn't want the usual customers to see us. We would be there at 8am, pick up our smack then head off for the day.

This was the beginning of my life and the end of my life. Everything revolved around heroin. For the first 6 years of my

[1] Buy Drugs

addiction, that's what I did; just turned up at the chemist every day. I never robbed anyone or hurt anyone. But in 1972, the government changed the regulations and brought out clinics. They started pushing methadone[2] on people and cutting down on prescriptions. That's when things really changed for us addicts. I quickly became addicted to methadone and started shooting up other drugs like diconal and barbiturates: drugs that aren't supposed to be injected. I developed a needle habit alongside my drug habit.

Everything spiralled out of control from there. I started losing friends nearly every week to heroin, through overdose or illness related to their habit. Some of my mates would contract pneumonia or septicaemia, but not bother going to the hospital for treatment. When you're an addict, you get to the point where you don't care about yourself.

The Black Market began to thrive as prescribed heroin diminished. Smack flooded the country from Iran, Cambodia and Vietnam. Each bag would have a little animal figure in it, like a white elephant, telling us which country it came from. From that time, we started breaking into chemists. They weren't alarmed in those days, so we would just steal the contents of the DDA[3] cupboard.

Because of my growing drug habit, I started doing crazy things. One time I was on the top deck of a bus during rush hour, with a needle hanging out of my arm, trying to start a fight with the

---

[2] Methadone is a pharmaceutical replacement for heroin, but just as addictive
[3] Dangerous Drugs Act

commuters. So the bus driver turned the bus around and drove me down to the Civic Centre, where I was thrown in a cell and later sectioned. I had no idea what I was doing!

I woke up in Knowle hospital (the local psychiatric hospital) covered in bandages. I was sectioned[4] under the Mental Health Act as a danger to myself and to the public for twenty eight days... they even took my clothes off me!

It was getting ridiculous! Friends around me were dying all the time. I was eventually banned from every clinic because I went on television to speak out against the government's new regulations. What the BBC didn't know, was that I took the £50 they paid me before the filming so I could score before appearing on the programme. I talked about how our psychiatrist wasn't really helping us and how I'd lost 3 friends that week alone. I guess I've always had it in me to speak up against injustice!

I remember this 24hour chemist in Piccadilly. It was crazy! At one minute past midnight, hundreds of addicts would turn up to collect their legal heroin. Then we'd all go down to the tube station toilets to shoot up. You could see the sinks stained red with blood from the needles we'd washed out. Drugs had arrived and they were staying.

The problem is, you can't stop an addict. A normal person is in control of their life, but an addict hasn't got any control: you don't have a say because every two hours you have to shoot up just to be able to walk around.

---

[4] Forced to stay in a psychiatric hospital

Finding the next fix became my life. So I decided, instead of robbing people I'd work for the Triads (a notorious Chinese gang) in London, pushing drugs. That way, I thought to myself, I could get top quality smack. I only dealt in half and quarter ounces of heroin, but it was enough to feed my habit. For the next three years, I supplied the addicts in Southampton with heroin, until I got busted at Waterloo Station...but that's for another chapter!

It might sound crazy to get involved with this gang, but they never threatened me as I never owed them money. Everything was done in cash. So my cash paid for their own addiction... gambling. Lots of them invested the drug money in takeaway restaurants. I knew one Triad who owned three takeaways within six months, one of which was in Chelsea!

They made money off drugs, but I never did, as every three bags I sold I'd take a bag myself. If I had been paying for my smack, it would have been a £300 a day habit! I figured being a dealer was safer than robbing people, as I was pretty unhealthy and well under weight. I never ate anything, only sweets and fizzy drinks. When you're an addict, you don't have an appetite.

My family didn't really know what was going on, no one did at that time. My mum even used to tidy all my gear in my room and put it on the bedside table! At first, they didn't realise how serious heroin addiction was. Then it got really bad.

I ended up clinically dead four times whilst on heroin: I heard voices in my head all the time, telling me to kill myself. Two weeks after I married my first wife, I did two weeks' worth of methadone in one hit. My parents and my wife had the vicar there reading me the last rites, but I woke up in the hospital. I had no idea what was going on, all I knew was that I needed a cigarette. So I ripped the IV drips out of my arm and headed for the door, not realising I had nothing on but a gaping hospital gown. I was there two minutes, before I was surrounded by doctors in white coats. I told them to give me my clothes back, I was off for a fix…

You see, heroin addiction is a whole lifestyle. It takes over everything. Every day you just get up in the morning and shoot up straight away, before you even get out of bed. Then all you can think about is where your next hit is coming from. On top of that you've got the police on your case all the time, drugs squad outside your house, you hear voices in your head… It makes you paranoid! Your life is chaotic and you're risking death every day, just for your next hit. You live a life of deceit, hiding the truth from family, friends… even from yourself. For the first 15 years I didn't want to come off heroin, but for the last 12, I was desperate.

Redemption Story

'By the blood of Jesus, I am redeemed
out of the hand of the devil.'

Things really changed for me in 1993. I was sleeping in my car in a place called Davidstowe, Cornwall. My marriage had broken down and my two kids were out of the picture. I was left with a clapped out car and a carrier bag of stuff - that was it. Addiction had taken everything else. I really wanted out of it. I was down to 7½ stone and the psychiatrist I was under in Plymouth was worried about me. She had thought I was going to die and said she'd make it easier; give me any drugs I wanted. Everyone, including myself, had given up on me. Except for Jesus, that is!

I felt so ashamed of the way I looked and everything about myself. I felt like a wire coat hanger; all my clothes just hung off me. I used to pick up my drugs then spend the rest of the day stoned on Bodmin Moor because I couldn't stand to be near anyone. You see, I was hearing voices in my head all the time and was completely paranoid. I was totally isolated.

So there I was, sleeping in my car, surrounded by thick Cornish fog, when I heard a tap on the window and this guy called Barry was smiling down at me. To begin with I thought it was the police, but I wasn't really worried as I knew they wouldn't search a car full of used needles. So I rolled the window down and he said, 'You look like you need some help. Do you want to come in? I'll give you a coffee.'

We crossed the road to where his house was, and in the garden I could see a huge wooden cross with lights, illuminating the A39. I told him I was living in my car and he said 'I've got a caravan across the road. Do you want to live there?'

And it was as simple as that; from that day on I lived in his caravan. Every day he would drive me to the chemist for my script, then make me a coffee and spend an hour with me, talking about Jesus and all the amazing things he has done. I didn't understand what he was talking about, as no one had ever told me. I knew there was evil in the world, as I saw it around me all the time, but I never really knew about this person Jesus. He started telling me that Jesus could change my life. Well, I had nothing to lose.

I had started going to church in Camelford with him and I met the Pastors, Ken and Hilda. Realising I needed some serious prayer, they fasted[5] for 40 days. It's funny, because they had no idea about addiction, but they did know Jesus could set me free! The week before I was finally free of heroin, a guy called Pastor David Chaudray had visited and prayed God would break the spirit of nicotine off me. I've never smoked a cigarette since.

Then came the day of my freedom from drugs.

The Christians that prayed for me that day gave me some declarations inspired by the blood scriptures; all about the blood of Jesus and his power.[6] They told me to read them out, so I started the first one '*By the blood of Jesus I am redeemed out of the hand of the devil*[7]', but when I got to the word blood, it felt like someone was strangling me and I sort of passed out.

An hour or so later, I woke up in a pile of mucus and vomit... but I was totally buzzing! I was so full of the Holy Spirit I thought I would burst! I was on fire for Jesus – I wanted to call up the

---

[5] Didn't eat any food and only drank water

[6] Blood Scriptures read over me that day - Psalm 107:2, 1 John 1:7, Romans 5:9, Hebrews 13:12

[7] Taken from Psalm 107:2

newspapers and tell everyone! I didn't have my junky head on any more – I was totally free in my mind. I snapped my needles and chucked the rest of my drugs down the toilet. I was free!

They told me later I had been delivered from 12 demons. It's funny, because that morning Barry had told me he'd had a dream about me, where he saw me fully clothed and in my right mind, sitting at the feet of Jesus. This was just like a guy in the Bible called Legion, who had been delivered from many demons and told by Jesus to return home and tell everyone what He had done for him.[8]

Later, this is exactly what God told me to do, to return to Southampton and never stop telling people what Jesus had done for me.

So that's what I do – Share Jesus with people every day. We've seen a lot of lives changed because He gives hope to people. It's about showing people there's hope; there is a way out of all this stuff. If Jesus can do it for me he can do it for anyone!

Within 18 months (1995,) I had moved back to the Flowers' Estate[9] in Southampton and was working in a homeless shelter, where I was trusted with the keys to the drugs cupboard. The staff and old addict friends asked me 'Don't you feel anything, Bob? Aren't you tempted?' And I replied 'I don't feel a thing, it's

[8] The story of Legion is found in Mark 5:1-20 and Luke 8:26-39

[9] The Flowers' Estate is a council estate, comprising housing funded by the Local Government

like I've never done heroin before.' That's what God did for me –
He gave me a new mind.

A few months before I started that job, a prophet[10] called Marc
Dupont said 'Bob, you've wondered if the chains from the past
are going to come back and drag you down again. But God's
told me to tell you, who the Son sets free is free indeed!' (John
8:36)

I had been given the keys to a cupboard full of methadone,
dexamphetamine, all the drugs I'd been addicted to, and I wasn't
even tempted. It was like I'd never even done drugs.

Some of the addicts in the hostel would throw bags of smack at
me trying to entice me, but the Holy Spirit[11] (the voice of God)
told me to turn around and walk the other way. Now my whole
life is reliant on the Holy Spirit: Listening to Him and doing what
He says.

Around this time I joined Hope UK (formerly The Band of Hope)
which was a Christian group, where people made a pledge not
to drink or take drugs. Through that group, I started doing
voluntary drug education all around Southampton and
Winchester.

I approached it differently from others. I never told kids not to

---

[10] A prophet is someone who often hears from God on behalf of other people

[11] The Holy Spirit is part of the Holy Trinity, comprising of Father, Son (Jesus)
and Holy Spirit. Jesus left Him with us here on Earth, as a guide and
protector. He is the part of God that speaks to us in our everyday lives. He
is in essence, the Spirit of God.

take drugs - I just told them my story. I explained how I had got into drugs and how bad it was, then how Jesus set me free. I still have grown adults tap me on the shoulder today and say they remember those talks, and all I'd been through, and stayed away from drugs as a result – Praise Jesus!

I even went back to my old school, where I had become an addict, sharing all about what God had done for me. He put me right back where I had started, so I could tell everyone about Him and His amazing love for us.

We had all sorts of discussions with the kids and the teachers about smoking and legalising cannabis! But I always felt the Holy Spirit was with me, touching people in those sessions. I remember doing a session at Westgate School in Winchester and loads of the pupils left at the end crying.

The Head teacher was curious and sat in on the next session. By the end, he just looked at me and said: 'You just keep doing what you're doing!' I knew it was the Holy Spirit working through me. They even wrote me a letter saying how special my time with the school was to them.

You see, young people need to know what a trap getting into drugs is. If you want to lose your freedom, then taking drugs is the way to do it! It's funny, because in the 60s we talked a lot about freedom: free love, free peace, freedom to take drugs... but by the end of the 60s we'd gone from hippies to stabbing each other in the back, trying to get more drugs.

The only real love, is the love of God. Our ideas were right, we used to protest against nuclear weapons and apartheid, but we were doing it in the wrong way. That was part of the reason I became an addict, I saw how messed up the world was and didn't think I could change anything. But with Jesus, I now know I can! He showed me when I became a Christian that we can change things in this world, but we can only change it with Him.

Through our work on the Flowers' Estate, I've been able to take various addicts to Christian Rehab. People are doing so well there. It shows them that a new life is possible, but it's only with Jesus! Two and a half years ago I took a couple of guys, John and Eccy, to a place called Yeldall Manor, a rehab set up and run by Christians.

John was a drinker and Eccy was a heroin addict. I'd been working with them for a few years leading up to this. I used to take food, and money for gas or electric to Eccy when he needed it. There's a lot of acts of kindness involved in seeing people really set free from addiction. You have to help people where they are, no matter how messy it looks! John used to come to our church meetings, with a can of beer in his hand and stand next to me when I was preaching. He'd say 'It's all gonna kick off Bob, I can feel the Holy Spirit!'

Anyway, both of them gave their lives to Jesus and that was the start of a new life for them really. We started talking about Yeldall Manor and how Jesus could set them both free from their addictions. We managed to get funding for them both to go for three months, but it took some faith.

The day before I drove John up, I rang Yeldall Manor and they said they were sorry but there was nothing left in the bursary. So we prayed, and when I phoned them the next day someone had paid a big chunk of money to them. Both men ended up staying there a year instead of three months!

They are now both clean, working in a Christian community with Christian support with their housing and every part of their lives. In the world you do 6-8 weeks of rehab, then you come out and go straight back to your old mates; your old life. But with God, it's a total change of lifestyle. Both John and Eccy have a completely new life because of what Jesus has done for them. They have a new Christian family that support and love them with the love of God, so they don't need to go back to their old friends.

It's what Jesus did for me and it is what he can do for anyone, anywhere, caught in addiction. If you want to know Jesus, you can say this prayer and let Him change your life:

Jesus come into my heart. Come and change my life and set me free. Come and be the Lord of my life. I believe you died on the cross for me and you were resurrected so I could have a new life. I confess with my mouth that you, Jesus, are Lord. In Jesus' name, Amen.

If you have said this prayer and meant it, God will show you His plan and purpose for you. It is the beginning of a new life with Jesus!

The Battle for My Mind

'Everyone wanted to see what had happened. They came up to Jesus and saw the madman sitting there wearing decent clothes and making sense, no longer a walking madhouse of a man.'
(Mark 5:14-15 The Message)

I was under psychiatrists for most of my life as an addict and was sectioned five times under the Mental Health Act. There weren't rehabs in the 70s, so if you wanted to get off heroin you had to go to a psychiatric hospital.

My first visit to Knowle Hospital was at age 17. They call it Knowle Psychiatric Hospital, but in my day it was known as the local lunatic asylum. My family pushed me to go in so I could get clean, but I wasn't really interested. I was just doing it to please people. I only stayed there two weeks and left with nothing but a prescription from my psychiatrist for more heroin.

My first memory of Knowle, was the long Victorian corridor painted in mental health green. I remember walking in and not being able to see the end of it. I felt afraid! I was on a ward called Redbridge and every type of person was in there, every type of mental illness you could think of.

There were people who would wake up in the middle of the night

shouting that they had a message from Mars. When the morning
staff arrived, the first thing they would do was check the toilets
for any suicides. If you've read *One Flew over the Cuckoo's Nest*
you'd have an idea of what it was like.

We were all drugged up to the eyeballs on Largatil; the liquid
cosh! We couldn't really go far. We'd be knocked right out on it;
parked in a chair all day. It meant they didn't need as many staff
to look after us.

They cut my heroin dose down over three days, but I was on so
much of the stuff at the time, that I ended up on cold turkey[1]. I
was on some drugs for the psychosis, but I was left on my bed
with shakes, vomiting and I couldn't even walk. I just lay on my
bed in the foetal position for days. I was ready to get out of there
though... I was already thinking about my next fix.

The next time I ended up on the psych ward was two years later,
to get my tolerance down. On my prescription I got four injections
of heroin a day, but soon that wasn't enough and I was shooting
it up all at once, just to stay normal. So I would check myself in
to Knowle, to get my tolerance down and give my body a little
rest. It meant the heroin would be more effective when I left.

By the time the clinics came out in 1972, I was addicted to

---

[1] Cold Turkey is a sudden withdrawal from heroin. It can cause restlessness,
shakes, severe aches, vomiting, diarrhoea, dehydration and severe depression.
It can also be fatal in long term users, as the body shuts down through shock.

barbiturates[2] and was sectioned, as a danger to myself and others. I was sent to a new facility, Ravenswood, in the grounds of Knowle. It was dormitory accommodation in those days, so we were all piled in together. You'd get so far coming off drugs, then someone would smuggle a bag of smack in and you'd be right back on it again.

I tried to get clean on my own a few times. In 1975, I'd heard about this hospital in London called Royal Bethlem in West Wickham – or Bedlam as it is better known! I remember they ran some tests on me. It was state of the art therapy in those days. They did CT scans and told me I had a lot of brain damage because I had done so many barbiturates and acid[3]. They said that once your brain cells die, you can't get them back – well that's what they say, Jesus says something else about that!

I went there twice and was voluntarily locked in with six other addicts. The first time I went, we were doing well, then a guy from Bude smuggled drugs in and we were straight back on it. The second time I tried, I met a guy called Billy from Romford and we ended up in West End for the night because we'd earned the right to come and go. I didn't want to mess him up, so I went off to score from some mates, but he did the same... When we came back the staff knew we had both used. They had packed our bags already!

---

[2] Barbiturates were originally used by doctors in the 1960s and 70s to sedate patients. However, they soon learnt they were very addictive and dangerous drugs that had damaging long term effects on the brain.

[3] A mind altering illegal substance

You met all sorts in Bethlem. One time I was in there, a member of the Royal family came in from Chelsea. He used to sit up and tell us all these stories about how he had smuggled morphine and heroin onto the Royal train travelling through Russia. When he got better he went down to Wickham to buy steak and made us all a slap up meal! He was a lovely bloke. People think addiction only affects a certain kind of person, but it can affect anyone. It's a powerful thing and you need something powerful to get you out of it.

I stopped going to mental hospitals when I was 30, but when they were introduced in 1972, I tried a few rehabs. As I walked in though I was offered drugs, so I just walked away. You see, a lot of people go to rehab because they are trying to get out of a court case. You're not ready in your mind, but the decision has been made for you, so you're not really serious about coming off the drugs. Then, you come out of detox, and just wait for something to go wrong, so you've got an excuse to go back to heroin... and so the cycle starts again!

I wasn't very popular with the staff in the hospitals I went to, because for the first 15 years I just wasn't interested in coming off heroin. I wasn't the model patient either, as I used to swap cigarettes for drugs off the other patients! Most of the time, in my mind, I was just paranoid and scared of the voices in my head, but you learn very quickly to hide the truth from psychiatrists and tell them what they want to hear. You don't care that you've just overdosed and could die, that seems like a good option at the time... but you never tell a psychiatrist that, or they won't let you out!

Looking back on it, I'm not fazed by people with mental health problems as I've seen so much of it in my own life. I've seen crazy things happen in hospital! I think the people who work in rehab clinics must get really frustrated because they don't see the results. People don't really have any answers. The problem with most modern rehabs, is that you only get funding for 8 weeks, then you return to your old life and old friends. Before you know it, you're back into addiction again. It's a vicious cycle. You can't get away from it.

I don't think people always understand that if you're an addict, you just don't have a say in your life. Rehab is often all based on will power, but I know Jesus can set you free and keep you free. I always knew deep down, that if I was going to live differently, I had to think differently – only God can totally renew your mind!

When I was an addict I had my 'junky head' on. Everything I looked at, I saw in terms of how much smack it was worth. Like the time I bought a £100 leather jacket in London, then sold it the next day for a £20 bag of heroin. Property doesn't mean anything to you, it's all just a way to get more drugs.

Or, I'd fill a syringe with the stuff and I knew it was too much, so I'd lie to myself and say I'll only do half. Then, when it was in my arm, I'd hear a voice in my head saying 'don't worry about it, just push the lot in.' So I did.

The only way you can renew your mind and change the way you think, is when you realise you need something more powerful than yourself. That's where God comes in!

Redemption Story

'Do not conform to the pattern of this world, but be transformed
by the renewing of your mind. Then you will be able to test and
approve what God's will is – his good, pleasing and perfect will.'
(Romans 12:2 NIV)

I knew something powerful had happened the day the church leaders prayed for me in Cornwall, because for the first time I wasn't lying to myself in my head. Jesus removed that 'junky head' and for the first time in my life I was being really honest. Even the day before, I had lied to the church, giving up a medicine bottle full of water to them, pretending it was my drugs, when really I'd just injected it all! Deceit becomes a way of life and you believe everything you're saying, but Jesus comes in and changes it. He changes your mind.

I now understand, that if I am going to help anyone, I need to first introduce them to their Maker. I've never met a medical person, in all my life, who can literally renew your mind, or change the way you think, but I know Jesus can. You just have to keep renewing your mind by reading His Word. When I came off heroin, I had to keep reading my Bible to find out what God thought of me, and I still do that every day.

When I returned to Southampton twenty three years ago, the police told me I wasn't welcome in the city, I was a waste of space. I could understand why they thought that, but I didn't think it anymore because I knew what my Father in Heaven said about me. It doesn't matter what people say about you, it's what God thinks that counts. He loves you and has planned good works for you to do!

When I came back to Southampton and joined Hope UK, I was invited back to Ravenswood. It had become a forensic psychiatric hospital by then, which means that people convicted of violent crimes related to their mental health were sent there. It was one step away from being sent to Broadmoor, a high security psychiatric prison. They'd asked me to do some drug education with a group of murderers.

While I was sitting there, I felt the Holy Spirit say 'look out the window.' I realised I was sitting in the same room I had first been sectioned in years before. I felt him say to me 'I've brought you back here, but you're free to go now.' It was like God was showing me, there's nothing He can't redeem in your life.

In everything we go through in life, there are moments God wants to use to help other people. God can use anything from your past – there's nothing He can't use for good. It doesn't mean you're living in the past, but you're using what you've been through and heading into the future! We had a good time that day. I shared my story about how I had come off drugs and how Jesus had set me free and it touched a lot of people.

The next time I returned to Ravenswood was about 10 years later, when a friend called Matty, from our Flower of Justice

Community[4], was sent there. He was on a section 41 (sectioned for life) for doing three armed robberies. I visited him every month, for seven years. I saw so many seasons come and go at Ravenswood during that time. It gave me many opportunities to share the love of Jesus with people!

It got to the point where Matty started bringing his three mates along, on day release, to our Flower of Justice Sunday services. They loved it! The nurses that accompanied them loved it too and I remember one lady telling me she always requested to take Matty on Sundays. All of the friends he brought along gave their lives to Jesus.

Visiting Matty also gave me the chance to share my story with the staff at Ravenswood. I remember one time, I was sitting in a room waiting for him to be brought up for his visit, and I had my Bible out. There was a psychiatrist, a nurse and two patients sitting in there with me.

One of the patients turned to me and said 'You're Matty's mate ain't you' and I said I was. Then he says 'You used to be in here didn't you?' I said 'Yeah, I was a patient here years ago.' 'Wow,' the other guy said 'you look like you're doing alright. Every time I get out I just go back to the pub and get angry... what's your secret?'

So I showed them 2 Corinthians 10 in my Bible, about taking every thought captive and explained that we are in charge of our thoughts and don't have to go with them. Then I showed them

---

[4] Charity set up to serve the needs of the community of the Flowers' Estate, Southampton

Romans 12: 2 about being transformed by the renewing of your mind and how living differently means thinking differently. I explained that it's only possible with God's help.

The nurse then piped up and said 'I've read the Bible and I've never seen that bit,' so I showed her too. Next, the psychiatrist says 'So there's a lot about the mind in the Bible?' So I explained to them that God says the real battle is in the mind and it's won or lost there. You can come off things physically, (drugs, alcohol, whatever your addiction is) but if you're not free in your mind, you'll never be free. It's amazing that just sitting in a room, waiting for my friend, I was able to do a Bible study and share the love of Jesus with people who wouldn't have heard it otherwise!

When God says in Isaiah 61:1 'I've come to set the captives free' He's not just talking about prisoners, but people trapped in their minds. You see, Jesus came to destroy the works of the Devil. The enemy wants to destroy human beings, whether you are a Christian or not. But, Jesus came to seek and save the lost; the people trapped in the prison of their minds. He died on a cross to rescue us from all the mess we've got ourselves in. He died for every mistake we've made… and every mistake we're going to make as well!

The last Christmas before they let Matty out, a psychiatrist stopped me and said 'I just want to thank you Bob for what you've done, coming in and talking to the guys in here. Do you realise what it is you're doing? They all know you are an ex patient and they see you come and go, free in your mind. You're giving them hope!' I hadn't even thought about it like that before.

To me, I was just following Jesus' command in Matthew 25:36 and visiting Matty in hospital. It's amazing how, if you let him, God can use every opportunity you have.

I've really enjoyed my time helping people with mental health problems. Flower of Justice still supports local people coming out of psychiatric hospitals, with food, help with bills and prayer. At the Men's breakfast we run, we have various people with mental health problems. One guy can scare people sometimes because he starts shouting at someone who isn't there. But it doesn't faze me or stop me helping anyone, because that was me once. He just needs people to care for him and love him.

God is always trying to give hope to people, even those that curse him. He's always saying 'look, there's a way out of this. I really care about you.' When I look back at my life, I realise I could still be in in a psychiatric hospital, sectioned. I remember glancing at one psychiatrist's notes, which said I was one of the most dangerous men he'd met! Words are powerful, they have life or death in them. But it's all about understanding what God says about you and living from that. It can all feel so hopeless, but Jesus has come to set us free and whom the Son sets free, is free indeed![5]

If you are struggling in your mind today, say this prayer with me:

'Heavenly Father, please set me free in my mind and help me change the way I think. Turn my negative thinking into positive thinking. Help me see myself the way you see me. In Jesus Name. Amen!'

[5]   Bible ref John 8:36

Prison

'I was in prison and you visited me'
(Matthew 25:36 NLT)

One day in 1972, I was on my normal three times a week trip to Gerrard Street, London. I was there to score Chinese heroin to deal in Southampton and keep my own habit going. As I approached the train in Waterloo, two drugs squad officers busted me and gave me a choice. They said: 'West End Central or Southampton Central?' I chose Southampton, because I knew the police in London were a totally different ball game; they were much tougher!

They found the heroin on me in Southampton Station. I had genuinely thought I could do a runner, as I had done many times before. But as I got off the train this time, there were 12 policemen waiting to escort me to a room upstairs. When they searched me they thought I had been ripped off, as I was carrying big lumps of smack, but they later found out it was 85% pure. I admitted to possession of ½ an ounce of class A drugs.

In those days, we had quarter Sessions so you'd have to turn up to four separate hearings, before your actual trial started. Mine was a big case. I'd already been on bail for 6 months, but by the grace of God, I was put in touch with Doctor Dale Beckett, who got me three years under Norwood Cottage Hospital, London. I believe he was one of the best psychiatrists around at the time.

It was the only hospital prescribing heroin at the time in the UK. Nearly everyone in there had lost a limb to heroin due to chronic infections from dirty needles. As they had been kicked out of everywhere else, this was the last clinic they could go to. So I ended up there.

When I turned up to the first quarter session, my barrister said there was nothing to worry about, it was just a preliminary, leading up to my main court case. However, within an hour they sent me downstairs to a cell, and half an hour after that I was in a van on the way to Winchester prison. I felt lucky I still had a little bit of my prescription left on me!

When you arrive at Winchester prison, you drive through double doors into a dark tunnel. Then you're searched. Next, you go through another set of doors, and through a massive razor wire gate, both of which are slammed shut behind you. Every step of the journey a door is shut behind you and you realise you are losing your freedom.

Because I had pleaded guilty, they put me in prison grey and took me to the hospital wing. I met a psychiatrist there, who took the rest of my heroin and tipped it down the sink, saying 'that's all you're getting in here, junky.' I was led to a padded cell. I was left alone, on cold turkey, for seven days.

I remember my dad was really concerned about my welfare, as

three of my mates had died from enforced cold turkey in Brixton prison, and no one was allowed to visit me. He drove all the way to the Home Office in London, to ask Ben Spear, a guy who worked in the Home Office Drugs Department, to help me. Ben knew some of us addicts from Southampton and he stuck up for me. He organised a visit for my dad half way through the week, to check I was ok.

After seven days, I was back in court again and put on bail. They took me to an office and in the corner I could see a big plastic bag, full of stuff. It turned out they had been picking up my heroin prescription for a week and now were giving it to me in one big hit. Then they said 'Do you get the message?'

I said 'I don't know what you mean.' 'You're not welcome in this city' one officer scowled 'you're leaving, one way or another.'

Eventually, I had my court case and my psychiatrist came down from London to speak up for me. He had so many letters after his name it was unbelievable! I had been charged with possession and conspiracy with 'unknown persons.' They didn't know who I was dealing for, so they couldn't pin anything on me.

I only pleaded guilty to possession, as I'd been caught bang to rights. I fully expected to be sent to prison, but my psychiatrist said if they sent me down they would be responsible for my death! So in the end I was put on eight years' probation instead, with the condition that I left the court and bought a one way ticket to London. If I returned to Southampton within three years, I would instantly be sent back to prison.

I was charged with conspiracy to deal in dangerous drugs and I could have been facing nine years in prison, but God saved me and only let me endure a week. I truly believe if I had been in prison any longer it would have broken me and I would have died there, like my three friends before me. But God had other plans!

God had his hand on me right throughout my eight years' probation and I can see it clearly now. The courts had wanted to send me on a new drug rehab programme called Alpha, which was all about breaking patients down then supposedly building them up again.

When I arrived there, the psychiatrist said I had to get on my knees and beg to come in. That was part of the programme which was meant to help people! I can't repeat what I said to him, but there were a lot of f's in it! I know now that God isn't about breaking anyone down, but building them up in love.

Also, for the first time in my life, I had a social worker and she really looked after me. She managed to find me a bedsit for £5 a week and a job at Design Display in Tooting, designing murals and artwork. I ended up designing a mural for Barking Library and one for WH Smiths in Nottingham.

The people at Design Display were good to me because they understood I needed time in the morning to shoot up in the staff toilet, before I could join them. I was with them for two years. It showed me I could work, as I hadn't had a job since I left school. It also showed me I could live a relatively normal life around other people who weren't addicts. Again, I believe God saved me from the Alpha programme and used something I was interested in (artwork) to help me.

Redemption Story

'The spirit of the sovereign Lord is on me, because the Lord has anointed me to proclaim good news to the poor. He has sent me to bind up the broken hearted, to proclaim freedom for the captives and release from darkness the prisoners.'
(Isaiah 61:1)

When I became a Christian and Jesus told me to return to Southampton, He spoke to me from Matthew 25 in the Bible; 'When I was in prison, you came to visit me… Whatever you do for the least of my brothers, you do for me[1]' So I just thought, I'll give this a go!

I met a lady back in 1993 called Betty Burke who ran the prayer group in Dartmoor Prison, and I joined them. She was an incredible woman. As well as being assistant to the Chaplain, she ran a hostel at the local Methodist Church, so women visiting the prison from all over the country had a place to stay overnight. She always made sure the inmates had plenty of Christian literature to read. I learnt so much from Betty! She later moved to Southampton to support me and Colette in our work on the Flowers' Estate.

---

[1] Matthew 25:36

I made up my mind that I wanted to do more prison work, as I was really enjoying it. Once I had completed my Prison Fellowship Training in Plymouth, I had a two year pass to visit prisoners under their guidance. It really taught me to work the way Jesus taught us. We always worked in pairs, covering each other's backs. Then at the end of each month, we would meet together as a team to talk about anything heavy from the inmates and pray for each other. It meant that none of us carried any burden alone.

Also, most of the people doing the training had had a tough life and been to prison themselves, so it felt like I was with other guys who really understood me. It's amazing how God was redeeming everything from our past, and now we were going back into prison, but it was totally different!

I think sometimes it's easy to go through your Christian life and not even notice that He's redeemed all parts of your life, for the good of other people. Nothing is wasted with God! When I talk to some people about my life, they say they are glad they didn't have to go through what I went through, and it's all very negative. But I totally disagree. When God redeems you, he takes back everything the enemy has stolen and gives you back even more. He uses what you go through to give you compassion for people in similar situations. That is what redemption is all about.

When doing my prison work, I used to give testimonies about all that Jesus had done for me. I really enjoyed it and found I had a lot in common with others, as most people in prison have had something to do with drugs.

When I returned to Southampton in 1995, I was invited to go into Winchester Prison by the Chaplain on a few occasions. He would just ring me ad hoc and say 'I've got 40 drug offenders here Bob, do you want to come and talk to them?' It was an amazing time and we saw many men give their lives to Jesus.

One service was in Leyhill Prison near Bristol. Me and a bloke called John were invited to do a service for lifers. John had been involved in the Strangeway Riots, but had given his life to Jesus. At the end of the service a Jamaican guy came up to me and asked me if I remembered him.

He reminded me of an incident in 1972, when I was rolled[2] by five men trying to steal my drugs. I'd had a knife on me, so I stabbed one of them, but luckily only got him in the arm. Well the Jamaican guy said, 'they rolled me the next day, but I stabbed one in the heart and now I'm in here doing life.' God showed me how that could have easily been me. He'd saved me from a life in prison.

I also remember another service I took at Winchester prison. I was in a bad way with Hep C[3] and my liver was really swollen. I sat in the car park and said to God, 'I'm gonna need you to help me here.' It was such a beautiful time. Many of the men gave their lives to Jesus and you could feel the Holy Spirit. I didn't

---

[2] Physically attacked for drugs

[3] **Hepatitis C** is a contagious liver disease that ranges in severity from a mild illness lasting a few weeks to a serious, lifelong illness that attacks the liver. It results from infection with the **Hepatitis C** virus (HCV), which is spread primarily through contact with the blood of an infected person.

really have to do anything, the Holy Spirit did it all! I even got to pray for two addicts at the end, who had started the service not believing I was even straight.[4] They left that service knowing Jesus was with them and they could face the world when they were released.

Sometimes people would see my testimony in Christian magazines or newspapers, so invite me along to speak at events. The Good News Paper printed my story. From that, I had an invitation from The Verne Prison in Portland, to speak at a Christian run part of the prison called Kainos Wing. Kainos, is Greek and it means 'new beginnings'.[5]

Incredibly, that wing only had a 4% re-offending rate. It had been the worst wing in the prison at one time, full of drugs and weapons. Then, some Christians stepped in to run it and all the wardens were believers from around the world. It's so funny, when you walk along the corridor there, you read scriptures on the wall and phrases like 'Jesus is Lord!' It is full of the Holy Spirit! They don't just work with the prisoners either, but with their families outside of prison. I was fortunate enough to get five of the guys I was working with in Winchester, transferred to Kainos Wing.

Also, living and working on the Flower Roads, I end up taking lots of families to visit relatives in prison. One guy (and good friend of mine) Milo, became a Christian whilst in Ford Open

---

[4] Drug free

[5] The Kainos Wing was opened in 1997 but, despite great success, was closed in 2001 amid political opposition about its overtly Christian ethos.

Prison and on the same day, his wife gave her life to the Lord in our front garden. Neither realised the other had made the step! I had the privilege of baptising the entire family when he was released.

Another guy called Manley, also gave his life to Jesus one day while I was visiting him in prison. I'd been praying for him for about 8 years, and I'd been to court with him on a few occasions. On one occasion, he was really up against it in court and I told him 'you won't get out of this without Jesus.' So we prayed and he was let off lightly by the judge. He believed in Jesus, but wasn't ready to let him into his life.

He was now serving four and a half years on a drug bust called Operation Phoenix, in Southampton. I had been taking his wife up to visit him, when I received a letter. In it, Manley simply wrote, 'I'm ready now.'

When I walked into prison that day, I could feel the Holy Spirit nudging me. So I said outright, 'Do you want to receive Jesus?' and he did. We prayed and he was in tears. It was beautiful. As I left the prison, I felt God remind me 'If you don't grow weary in doing good, you will reap a harvest.'[6] Funnily enough, two of his daughters also became Christians in prison. God has his hand on the entire family!

You see, Jesus came to set the prisoners free. Whether that is the prison of drugs, mental health problems or actual physical bars around you. It is so important to Jesus that we continue to

---

[6] Galatians 6:9

visit prisoners, otherwise he wouldn't have mentioned it in Matthew 25. God loves the prisoners!

I remember God saying to me in court once, 'how will I reach these people if no one will sit and listen to them?' God pursues the prisoner because he wants to set them free. We need to remember those in prison and realise that it can be used for good. Prison can be a special time for people and many people give their lives to Jesus whilst in prison. It can be a time when things are turned around for people. We must always remember those who are in prison and pray for them. After all, it could easily be any one of us in their shoes.

If you are in prison or know someone who is, pray this prayer with me now:

'Heavenly Father, I ask that you would help me to live a different life. I ask you Lord Jesus to come into my heart, into my life, and change everything for me. I believe that you came to set the prisoners free and I ask you to set me free inside and out. I ask you to help me live a new life. In Jesus name, Amen.'

Speaking up for Others

'Speak up for those who cannot speak for themselves;
ensure justice for those being crushed.'
(Proverbs 31: 8-9 NLT)

As an addict in Southampton, the police would pick me up in the High Street on a regular basis and take me to the cells. It was easy to pick on me as I was as skinny as anything, but I think they were fed up with me. I was dealing in heroin, just so I could get my own. I never made any money, but I was despised by the police and the courts. They all knew my name!

When I turned up in court the judge would normally look at me and I could tell they were thinking, 'Oh no, it's him again!' You see, I used to go to court on my own and had no one to speak up for me. Most of the time I was out of it anyway. I used to bring friends to court sometimes, but they'd be so out of it too that they'd get kicked out. Most of the time they'd just sit in the gallery and laugh at me because I was getting it all wrong on the stand. But I didn't care.

At the time, we were into two comedians called Cheech and Chong, who were big on the drugs scene. They did funny sketches about tripping out and smoking cannabis. One sketch they did, called 'Tripping in Court,' involved a man accused of taking LSD claiming he'd only done it 25 times!

So the time I got busted for having large amounts of heroin, my friends thought it would be funny to come along and trip out in the Gallery. They couldn't stop laughing, as the judge was asking me a load of questions and I was talking rubbish. I was talking about something completely different! In the end, the judge had my mates sent out and the Hearing postponed until I was in a more fit state to attend. My so called friends weren't there to support me, they'd just come for a laugh.

As I said, the only person who spoke up for me in that case was Dr Beckett. He used to really look after us addicts. My dad used to speak up for me too, but he couldn't take time off work to come to court. I didn't want my family involved in any court cases. I'd got myself into a mess, so it wasn't up to them to sort me out.

In my head, I could justify everything I was doing. I was incapable of really caring about anyone: I had no conscience, no friends. Even though people were always looking for me to buy drugs off, I was quite a loner.

That's one thing heroin does to you; it becomes your everything. You talk about it like she is your lady. She meets your needs 365 days a year, even on Christmas! I believed I would never cope on my own in this world, without heroin. This attitude made me even more isolated. I would go in to town, do my business then disappear.

I did things I'm not proud of. Once I brought a Chinese guy down from London and put him up in a house in town. His name was Tommy. At the time, I was visiting London 3 or 4 times a week, but it was getting really hot[1] on Gerrard Street (China Town) and the police were all over us. So I moved Tommy down to Southampton, just because it made it easier for me to get my drugs.

I said to him, 'You can make more money if you move to Southampton and I'll get you a load of customers.' He was a young guy and he was getting a lot of bother from the police. So he went for it and I moved him into a bedsit, not far from where I was staying.

I used to see Tommy every day, near enough. We used to go to London together to see his bank manager – an old Chinese guy with suitcases full of money! Although I saw a lot of him, I wouldn't say he was my friend; more of a business associate. I didn't really have any friends. The police at West End Central knew my face. I was in trouble, so I used Tommy to get myself out of it.

You see, all of your values go out the window when you're an addict. I used to say I wouldn't sell to young people, but I did. I got busted by the drug squad once, but I was sick and in such a bad way I didn't really know what was going on.

I'd been walking down Fanshaw Street in Southampton, on my way to pick up my drugs from the Mental Health Clinic, when a

---

[1] Lots of police activity/presence

young guy approached me to buy some gear. I wasn't planning to rip him off or anything, I just told him to come with me and wait on the corner, while I got a couple of bags off Tommy.

When I got back and handed him the drugs, out of the corner of my eye, I noticed two guys running at me. It was the drug squad! So I started legging it down the road, but they caught up with me, rugby tackling me to the ground. Turns out the guy I was selling to, was only fifteen years old.

I didn't realise he was so young – to be honest, I didn't think about it. Your standards just slip when you are on heroin. You become so self-focused you don't really care about anyone else.

After that, Tommy moved back up to London because things were getting difficult with the police. I didn't want to land him in trouble, so I guess I had a bit of a conscience on that one!

My habit was in control of my life. To have a habit, you've got to feed it. That's what I learnt when I became a Christian; what you feed becomes your habit. Even with other stuff, like pornography, if you feed on it, it soon becomes a habit. It can be a dangerous place to be in. Repentance though, is all about changing your mind and walking away from the harmful thing you've been doing.

As a heroin addict, you are considered the lowest of the low... Even the alcoholics who dealt me my barbiturates looked down on me! When I was injured by the police in West End Central, and my dad went to speak up for me, the officer told him 'Your son doesn't have any rights, he's a junky!' People look down on you, just because of who you are. Most addicts have death around them anyway. They don't care whether they live or die. But that's who Jesus came for, the lost and broken!

That's why, in my work on the Flowers' Estate now, I always stick up for addicts even when they go back to drugs. I was continually being judged by people, so it's important for me to be in a place where I don't judge anyone. It doesn't matter who they are or what they've done.

Jesus' last commandment was love one another and that is what we are supposed to do. If you see a brother in need and you don't help him, the Bible says you haven't got the love of God in your life (1 John 3:17.) That's quite a frightening thought really, but it is the heart of God. The Holy Spirit lives inside us, and He is love. We see it on the estate every day. If you ain't got love in your heart, you ain't got anything.

It can feel like my old life was a waste, and it was, but when God came into it every experience was turned round for the good. He can do that for any one of us, if we are willing to let Him. Even the mistakes I make now, in my Christian life, are there so I can help other people and stay humble. God can't stand it when we're self-righteous and think we've got it all together! It's true that pride comes before a fall[2] and we must never forget where we've come from.

---

[2]   Proverbs 16:18

My Nan and my Aunty with me on Bournemouth beach.

Me with my Mum and siblings on Mudeford Beach, in the 50's. Left to right: Barry, Mum, Steve, me, and Sue.

Me on a junior school trip to Wimborne Miniature Village, Dorset.

My grandparents on my Father's side. My Nan was the only Christian in my family when I was growing up.

Me, as a teenager, at the beginning of my drug habit.

Knowle Hospital, Fareham, Hampshire.
The place I was first sectioned.

Mrs Whitehouse's home, Lesnewth, near Boscastle.

Some of the sheep I tended for Mrs Whitehouse.

A picture of me with my first Bible, when I was newly saved in 1993.

Me on a visit to Downinny Mission, where I first gave my life to Jesus

*Me with Dave and Tina, two good friends
who met Jesus at the same time as me.'*

*Me with my dear pastors Ken and Hilda.
Without them, I would not be here today*

My beautiful wife Colette, and me, on our wedding day, 3rd September 1996 at Central Hall, Southampton.

Some members of our Flowers Christian Community.

My dear friend and mentor, Gary Stache.
His support and friendship means so much to me.

My wife Colette and me on holiday in California,
provided by our good friend Gary.

Redemption Story

'When you are brought before synagogues, rulers and
authorities, do not worry about how you will defend
yourselves or what you will say, for the Holy Spirit
will teach you at that time what you should say.'
(Luke 12:11-12 NIV)

The first time I spoke up for someone in court was when I
was working in the hostel. It was a young guy called
Steve, who was up on charges for shoplifting. I'd been
working closely with him and we planned to help him get off
drugs, once the case was over. I spoke up for him and explained
that, as his key worker, I could help get him into rehab. The
charges were dropped and Steve did well for a time. Sadly, he
later returned to drugs and they took his life. He knew the Lord
before he died though and I am confident he is in His hands now.

Through this first experience, God reminded me how difficult it
is to stick up for yourself in court and how important it is to speak
up for others. It's helpful to have someone with you who knows
they aren't going to prison! Gradually, I went to court with more
and more guys from the hostel. The courts got used to me and
started to accept me as an advocate. This was great training for
the work that was to come on the Flowers' Estate!

As part of my work on the Flowers' Estate now, I often go to court
with people and speak up for them. I don't condone what they
have done, but you can see when people are faced with a fine

for example, it's going to cripple them. Plus, they would be back in court in 6 months' time anyway, for non- payment. So we see God move on their behalf and many times we've seen fines dropped.

It's also about peace keeping in the court too. Some of the people I help represent, can be quite vocal in court, but because I am there and we pray together, Jesus gives us His peace and gets us through it. He helps us to keep quiet and not upset the judge! I've got to know a lot of the solicitors at Southampton court over the years, and they tell me it's made it easier for them too. The courts know who The Flower of Justice are, so I'm often invited to speak up in court or write a letter outlining a family's financial position. It's a great privilege really.

You'd be amazed how mentioning the name Jesus in court, changes everything. I often feel pressure in the witness box, thinking they'd laugh at me if I talk about Jesus, but I've learnt not to care. I'll stand there and say 'Jesus has changed this person's life, Your Honour!' Then the court goes quiet and all eyes are on me! But we've seen miracles happen in court, where the judge has completely softened because they don't usually get good news. And I've had prosecutors, who have been totally against what I'm trying to do with a person, turn around and shake my hand saying 'that was real justice, Bob!'

One time a lady called Yvonne (a woman from our Christian Community) had been done for assaulting a police officer. She never actually hit anyone, but the police had turned up to arrest her son and were really putting the boot in, so she got in between them. She was on a conditional discharge[3], so was facing time in prison for it.

When it went to court, I remember she had one of the hardest judges in the court system! She knew the family name and didn't look happy. She'd been dealing with her family for the last 20 years. The court allowed me to speak on Yvonne's behalf, so I told them I was her pastor and that she had given her life to Jesus. I even told them about the Bible studies we were having in her house!

Anyway, the judge was really poker faced throughout. I've worked with this judge quite a few times, and people don't usually just walk out of there. But when she came back in from deliberations, she had a smile on her face. She said, 'This is the best news I've heard this year! As Mr Light has spoken up for you, I can see that you are not in a financial position to pay a fine, so the court will not be charging you. I also think we can drop the conditional discharge. You're free to go.' It was so funny because Yvonne had her packed carrier bag with her... she thought she was going to prison there and then. She couldn't believe she was free to leave!

Another young woman we knew, called Leoni, was in trouble for drug dealing. She was busted with her dad, but I knew she wasn't involved, she had just given him a lift. The police were conducting an investigation called Operation Phoenix. It was a tight operation and the police were going for everyone involved.

---

[3] An order made by a criminal court whereby an offender will not be sentenced for an offence unless a further offence is committed within a stated period.

If you were caught, you were looking at a minimum of 4 years in prison. So Leoni got done for it.

On the day of her Hearing, they transferred her down from Bronzefield Prison up in London, to the Magistrates court in Southampton. I was sat at the back with all these crack dealers and I was getting really fed up of listening to them go on about their prison time and drugs. Then I was asked to speak, so I started speaking up for Leoni.

I told the court we'd known her since she was 12, that she'd come to Club Zion (our youth club) and we were working with her family. I felt the Holy Spirit say the judge was listening to me... and then it went ballistic! The prosecution could see the Judge was going to give her bail, when nobody arrested on Operation Phoenix was allowed it.

Next thing, a guy from the Drug Squad had hold of my arm and was asking for my date of birth, whilst on the phone doing a police check on me... all while I was talking! You've got to understand, I'm still a registered heroin addict and my last conviction was conspiracy to deal heroin. So he's stood there getting all this information on the phone, when the crack dealers at the back pipe up and start shouting 'leave him alone! Can't you see God's changed his life?!' She still wasn't allowed bail, but God had other ideas...

Finally, on the day of the Trial, Leoni turned up to Court with nothing but a Bible in her hand. The Judge said to me 'Mr. Light, you're her pastor, tell us a bit about her then.' So I told the Judge all about what Jesus was doing in her life and how she had changed since the bust. I could tell he was really listening to what I had to say.

Then the prosecution turned round and said 'Well your honour, after what she's been involved in she should really be serving 4 years in prison, but after hearing Mr. Light and for the fact that she's already served one, if she serves another month she will have done enough time.' So Leoni returned to prison and was released after only a few weeks. Instead of serving 4 and a half years, she only served 1!

At the end of the Hearing, the prosecutor shook my hand and said 'That was real justice, Bob!' You've got to understand that God is a God of justice and it's not the sort of justice we think of. God's interested in people's lives and he knows what they need. If He can change the mind of a King like a river[4], He can do the same with a Judge. I've always believed that and I've always seen that.

Another case that really stands out in my memory, is a neighbour who got done for £4,500 of Benefit Fraud. He became a Christian with us at Dip week, our annual community week, then told us he had to go to court soon. He tragically lost his partner six months before and he was in a bad way. He was a window cleaner, so his work was seasonal, but he hadn't been signing off during the times he was working.

So I went to court with him and I remember saying 'I don't think

---

[4] Proverbs 21:1

you're going to get away with this, unless we pray now and ask Jesus.' So we prayed right there, outside the court. When the Judge asked me to speak, I said I was his pastor and I told him basically what I knew about him. The Judge then did something unusual. He said 'I'm not going to make a decision about this now... there's something different about this case. Come back at 2pm.'

It's weird, because that morning I had really heard the Holy Spirit talking to me when we were in court. He said 'you've done well, you've loved this guy and you know a bit about him. But there's one thing I need to remind you, I know everything about him.'

When we came back that afternoon, the Judge didn't even give us a chance to sit down. He just said 'I don't know why I am doing this, but you're completely pardoned.' I was shocked. Then I heard the Holy Spirit speak to me and He said 'Why are you so surprised? I pardoned you, why wouldn't I pardon him?' So I learnt a lesson that day.

Speaking up for people isn't just about representing them in court, it's also about taking a stand against bullying or badmouthing. I remember in the hostel there was this one alcoholic guy who was getting a mouthful in the Pool room from three skinheads. They were winding him up so he'd leave the room, calling him a boozer and other insults. In the end, he got so upset, he smacked one of them with a pool cue!

I was in charge that day, so they came round to the office to complain to me and get him kicked out. When he told me his side though, I refused. They had been bullying him and I knew it wasn't his fault. I knew the guy well and I believed him. I could hear the others laughing at him.

Next day, I was summoned into the office by my manager. I walked straight into a kangaroo court! They were all there, the three skinheads and senior staff, sitting round the table looking at me. The Holy Spirit said to me 'Don't speak! Don't say a word!' So I sat down and listened to them accuse me of not doing my job properly and letting a guy stay after he'd assaulted someone.

I really wanted to say something, but God kept telling me to keep quiet, so I did. Gradually, the three guys started to get so frustrated that the truth came spilling out of their own mouths. They started swearing and saying things like they didn't want drinkers in the hostel. It was really nasty! But I stayed silent, then when it was over, got up and walked out.

My manager ran after me and apologised. She said 'I'm so sorry Bob, we should have believed you. What are you going to do?' I was angry, so I wanted to say I was gonna jack it in and quit, but then she said 'how will you ever change things, if you leave?' Well that got me. God had put me there and I was staying until he told me to leave.

You see God's involved with the whole thing about advocacy. He wants us to speak up for those who can't speak up for themselves and He'll give you what you need to do it. He wants to see His sort of justice served. He gives people what they need, not what the world says they deserve. Jesus is the most merciful person you will ever meet! If He's pardoned me for all I've done in my life, I know He can pardon anyone.

If you, or someone you know is facing a court case, pray this prayer with me now:

Jesus, I thank you that you are a God of Justice and your kind of Justice isn't like the world. I ask you to have mercy on my situation and lead me through it in your love. Thank you that every sin is pardoned by the power of your blood and you speak up for me when I can't speak up for myself. Amen

Acts of Kindness

'Do not let kindness and truth leave you.
Bind them around your neck.
Write them on the tablet of your heart.'
(Proverbs 3:3 NASB)

During the 1970s I was the main dealer of heroin and other substances in Southampton. My life revolved around travelling to London, making up bags every day and selling them to keeping my own habit going. I went down this road where I didn't really care about or love anyone. I had no conscience. I think most addicts live like this just to keep themselves going.

As an addict, you become a good hustler, which means you get really good at ripping people off! Sometimes you would work with another addict, to hustle people so you could get more money.

One time, I was dealing with some customers from Chichester. They wanted 5 or 6 lbs of cannabis, which was worth a lot of money! So I drove them over to a friend's house and told them to wait in the car. Then I came back out and said 'look mate, he ain't just gonna lay the dope on me, unless you pay up front.' They handed over the money, so we just walked out of the back door and jumped in a taxi to the train station, headed for London. There was no cannabis, we just needed the cash for our next fix!

Every day I looked for opportunities to scam people. I remember I had a regular come down from Bath and they had about £5,000 on them to buy gear. In my mind I thought 'I'm gonna get that money!' So I took them to a pub and pretended there was a dealer inside. Again, I told them to wait in the car and when I came out said, 'There's no way this guy is going to deal with you. Give me the money, put me in a taxi and I'll get your drugs for you.' So they did, and I went straight to the station again, heading for London.

You see money like that doesn't mean anything when you're an addict. I just blew it all in a few days, staying in London hotels and doing things I shouldn't do. You justify everything in your head and deal with the consequences afterwards, if you have to. Some people take hustling too far though and have to leave town as so many people are after them! You can't hustle too much.

I remember one guy at Piccadilly Station, had a suitcase full of drugs he'd nicked from a chemist. Again, in my head I thought 'I'll have that case within an hour.' I wasn't in a physical state to beat him up or anything like that, so I worked out a scam. I could see he was nervous hanging around there and was desperate to shift the stuff. I said to him 'Look mate, you're gonna have to trust me with this. Give me the suitcase and I'll take it to someone I know who's got the cash up front.' Boom - That was it. I was gone. Got the Tube and didn't look back.

Addicts had different skills when it came to hustling and we used them to our advantage. I knew guys who were excellent pick pockets and could strip you of your wallet on Oxford Street within seconds. I also knew addicts who wore pin stripe suits and pretended to be businessmen to scam doctors for drugs. They would say they were travelling salesmen and had forgotten their prescriptions. Amazing how many people fell for it!

I hustled with women a lot too, so I could pretend I was their husband, as people were more likely to believe us. We would change the format all the time. We lived in squats, but pretended we were paying rent so the government would give us money. We even had fake rent books!

Once, we knew the local council were coming round to inspect the place, so we painted it. Then my mate nicked a lawn mower from 3 houses down. When they showed up, there he was, busy cutting the grass! The guy from the council commented 'You've got a nice place here.' He just fell for it and believed we were legitimate tenants. I don't know how we pulled that one off!

I was in London all the time, and The West End was an easy place to scam people. The pace of life is so fast there. Right from when you arrive at the Dilly[1] to pick up your prescription, there's stuff going on. There used to be a circle in Piccadilly Tube Station that all us addicts stood around in. Everyone was off their head on something – There was nothing you couldn't buy there! You had to have money to get drugs though, so you would hustle. There was one guy in Covent Garden who owned a hot dog stall. If you

---

[1] Piccadilly Circus

got there early enough, he'd let you take it out and sell drugs under the counter!

You get paranoid as a dealer, as you usually have people looking for you. You end up mixing with people you really shouldn't be mixing with. I remember we were staying in a flat overlooking Earls Court, London. We were living and dealing from there. One day we heard a knock on the door and two guys appeared with baseball bats. They were part of the Kray gang! They wanted £200 off us, to carry on dealing on their patch. We just paid it. You didn't mess with the Krays!

Another time, there was an aircraft carrier docked in Portsmouth, with 5000 men on it. A lot of people at the time didn't realise that Americans would join the navy so they didn't go to prison for drug offences. They'd been given the choice by the courts.

Anyway, all our local pubs would close by 11.30pm, but I met a lot of sailors down there and could get them into the Jungle[2] late at night. I'd sell smack to them to keep my own habit going. I never really thought twice about it.

I also used to do a lot of business with the Hell's Angels on the south coast. They had a couple of factories where they produced speed. They dealt in stolen cars too. But this was all just part of normal life for me!

One night at about 2am, me and a mate did over a chemist, in a little town not far from Southampton. He was so skinny, he fitted

---

[2] Also known as 'The Area' in Southampton, where drug addicts hang out.

through the bars to let me in! He had ripped the DDA cupboard off the wall and was emptying the contents out, when a light came on in the flat above.

I was just stood there holding a jemmy[3]. He said, 'If anyone walks in, hit them over the head with it!' I knew it would've killed someone, but I didn't really care. It's only by the grace of God that I didn't end up murdering someone that night.

We drove through the New Forest that night, with the Police right behind us. We off roaded it and they didn't bother following. I think we ended up just staying out under the stars for a few weeks. We had enough drugs to keep us high! It made us paranoid being out in the open. It wasn't good.

I kept thinking I could see the Drug Squad coming out of the dark. We were arguing a lot too, because we would stash stuff for later, then forget where we had hidden it. In the end, I got my mate to drop me at Brockenhurst Station, where I just sat under the light. My mind was wrecked.

You don't have a conscience when you're an addict: ripping people off is a normal part of life. Even when your friends are in trouble, you just have to leave them. You don't care who you rip off or what you've done to them. All you can think about is heroin, and where your next fix is coming from. That's all that matters to you. This sort of life is a dead end. You can't see a way out of it.

---

[3] Crow bar

I know sometimes I sold drugs to people and they died. I'm not proud of it. It was the risk you took as an addict. You never know if you are shooting up 'good' stuff, or if it's been cut with something nasty. People are really messed up when they're drug dealing. I saw one guy putting battery acid in heroin. Another dealer would put brick dust in his. You're living in a different world and evil is all around you. You don't really care about anything, you just want to keep your habit going.

I saw how hard I had become because people would die around me and I didn't feel anything. One guy died next to me in a squat, so we wrapped him in a carpet and left him in the garden. We didn't want the police to think it had anything to do with us.

Another time, I was shooting up with an addict in a toilet cubicle and he turned blue in front of me. I just had to leave him there and climb out, or I could have been done for attempted murder. You do things that you would never normally do in your right mind.

During this time when I was dealing and hustling, I had several experiences with the police where I had nothing on me, but they would still rough me up a bit. I remember my dad going to West End Central, and complaining to the Chief Inspector about the way I had been treated. He just said 'This son of yours isn't a human being, he's a junky and he has no rights.'

People often see heroin addicts through a lot of misinformation. They don't realise the person in front of them is a human being and they're not in control of their lives. They're doing what they're doing because of the drugs, not because they want to. They don't have kindness in their lives, so they don't know how to show it to others. But Jesus changed all of that for me!

Redemption Story

'Is not this the kind of fasting I have chosen:
to loose the chains of injustice
and untie the cords of the yoke,
to set the oppressed free
and break every yoke?
Is it not to share your food with the hungry
and to provide the poor wanderer with shelter -
when you see the naked, to clothe them,
and not to turn away from your own flesh and blood?
(Isaiah 58:6-7 NIV)

Now I have a life in Jesus which is totally opposite! Where I was peddling death before, now I'm dealing in acts of kindness. I noticed straight away when I became a Christian that I was developing a conscience too: I just couldn't do half the things I used to do. As an addict, it never entered my head to do an act of kindness. I think I believed what one psychiatrist had told me, which was that I was incapable of loving. But God started helping me to love the way He loves.

I remember the first Christmas I was a Christian, I really wanted to do something to help others. So I volunteered to serve food to lonely people in Camelford Library. I got so much out of doing it. It really fulfilled me, so I started thinking about ways I could help people. I'd never cared about myself, let alone anyone else when I was an addict. But God taught me He loves everyone, so it doesn't matter who I meet, I know God loves that person. That's a certainty! He loves everyone He created.

A lot of people have never experienced going without, or not having enough food in the house. But both my wife, Colette, and myself have been on benefits in the past, so we know that when you're on benefits there's at least two days in the week where you don't have any food in the cupboard.

So God showed me 'You're either part of the problem or part of the solution' and 'judging people doesn't help anyone.' It's unreasonable to say someone has done something wrong, so they don't deserve help, as you never know their full story. It's so important for people to feel part of God's family and accepted as they are. Addiction is such a selfish lifestyle, but God can turn you right around.

God tells us to deny ourselves, pick up our cross and follow Him. That means putting others in your life first!

When we first moved onto the Flowers' Estate, we prayed a lot and God showed me that He really cares about those who are struggling with not having enough food. In Isaiah 58 it says we should feed the hungry and look after people. So we started a food project.

It started off really small. I was working with families (through our kids work) and lots of parents wanted to talk about debt they were in. Payday loan companies prey on families with low income, who need money in the short term but can't pay the high interest. It's all to keep marginalised people, marginalised. It's really corrupt. I was praying about it and God showed me it was impossible for families to repay their debts and put food on the table. Colette and I realised, we could negotiate a manageable amount to repay with the bailiffs, but we would need to feed people in order for them to keep it up.

One of the first families we helped had 11 kids, living in a 3 bedroom house. I used to just buy them food to begin with, out of my own money. Then we had other Christians join us prayer walking the estate, who would help us out. A dear lady called Peggy Escott would buy an extra bag of shopping every week and donate it to our work. Then a family from Community Church Southampton, the Judds, started buying three or four bags of shopping for us every week too. So it just started off really small and built up as God provided.

Over the course of a few years, it grew to 15-20 families a week, as God gave us more money. We would do the shopping at ASDA, then I'd drive round in my car delivering it to families in need. We worked out that for a set amount of money, we could feed a family for five days a week, so they'd only have to find the money to buy two days' worth. That meant they could pay off their debts, but it also left them a bit for Gas and Electric each week.

However, as the price of food went up, we had to start helping people with fuel poverty. I would be called round to a family at night and the whole family would be sitting on the stairs in darkness because they'd no electricity. This sort of thing happens all the time on the estate. It's poverty behind closed doors. So we'd help them out by putting a bit of money on their key. It also gave us the opportunity to pray with people and journey with them.

The food project today looks totally different. We buy food from a charity called Fareshare and I also get given free food from Tesco twice a week. They'd like us to do more! I think super-markets are ashamed of their food wastage. So much of it goes in landfills, but things are changing…

I also think it's a sign of the times that so many people are using food banks in this country. There is so much need today. Benefits are cut, people are being evicted; families are desperate. You've got to understand everyone's situation is different, so you can't judge anyone. It'd be ok if there was work available, but many of the people we help struggle to find work due to circumstance or past convictions. We can't change what the government's doing, but we can change people's circumstances.

It can seem overwhelming, but you have to just help the person in front of you. We've helped pay courts amounts of money to prevent families being evicted. We buy school uniforms and shoes for kids starting a new year at school. We've sponsored children in gymnastics clubs and football teams. We've even sent two children to a private Christian School, fully paid, as they were being so badly bullied at their local school! We've taken kids to Soul Survivor[4] and families to Lee Abbey[5], all for free.

All along the journey, God has provided for the work on the estate, through generous people who believe in God's vision for this place. We've never counted up how much He has given us over the years, but I am sure if we did it would be a huge amount. And every penny of it went directly to the people we were serving…His is an incredible God who provides for His children!

If you want to know God and show His kindness in your life, say this prayer with me now:

'God, I thank you that you show endless kindness to me. Please help me to be more like Jesus and show kindness to all those around me. Soften my heart and give me an opportunity to show your kindness every day. Amen.'

---

[4] A Christian Summer Youth Camp

[5] A Christian Retreat in Devon

Physical Healing

'Then your light will break forth like the dawn,
And your healing will quickly appear;
Then your righteousness will go before you,
And the glory of the Lord will be your rear guard.'
(Isaiah 58:8 NIV)

As well as receiving freedom from addiction, God has given me healing in my body. When you're addicted to heroin, you don't want to go to hospital when you get sick, in case they cut your prescription off. I had friends who died of pneumonia and septicaemia because they left it too late to see a doctor.

I had hepatitis twice, with jaundice at the same time, so my eyes used to be banana yellow. The first time I had it I was still an addict, so I didn't go to hospital. It must have been Hep B, because years later when I was tested for it at my job in a hostel, I already had an immunity to it!

The second time I was diagnosed however, in 2000, it was labelled Hep C. I had to go back to injecting myself with a drug called interferon for my treatment, which I didn't like doing, but was glad it was only skin deep and not in my veins. I had been on it for 9 months and it had made me clinically depressed as well as physically unwell. I knew it was fighting my disease, but I didn't like it one bit!

It was a week before Christmas when we were called in to see the consultant. He told us the interferon hadn't worked and I had a year to live. When you have Hep C, they give your liver a score out of 10 and if it scores below 5 you've had it, you are going to die. Well I scored 4!

This might sound like devastating news, but God had spoken to me that morning and said 'whatever they tell you, I just want you to trust me.' The registrar was a young guy and he was really nervous, so I tried putting him at ease. I wasn't afraid because of what God had said! Even when you get a negative report from the doctor, it's about remembering God's bigger.

As I walked out of the hospital, I heard a little voice say to me 'Where's your God now?' I knew it was the enemy and I knew my God was with me, living inside me. He had brought me this far and I would have been dead years ago any rate, if it wasn't for Him. I had nothing to lose really! I trusted God completely.

In the year that followed, I shared my testimony with everyone I could at the Infectious Diseases Unit of the hospital. The waiting room is like a goldfish bowl, so it's perfect for sharing about Jesus! Every nurse, doctor and consultant I spoke to, heard my testimony. The Holy Spirit was really moving there.

God used that time to teach me things too. I had lost most of my teeth to heroin[1] when I was younger, but the eight that remained needed to come out. So the hospital made an appointment for me in the dental unit.

Well, the woman at Reception started shouting at me saying 'We can't treat people like you here. It would take four hours just to clean the room for infection!' I just started walking out of the hospital because I didn't want to stick around. Then this Sister came running after me, apologising, saying it shouldn't have happened and invited me back in.

So I returned with her, and they asked me if I was off of drugs now. It gave me the perfect opportunity to tell her about Jesus! The next thing, she goes to get this Egyptian guy, who turned out to be a dentist. He also asked me how I came off heroin, so I told him about Jesus too. He thought it was fantastic what had happened to me, and apologised again for the way I had been spoken to.

He then told me I'd have to have my teeth out in the IDU , in isolation, as Hep C is contagious and they couldn't risk it. Other patients at the IDU include patients with AIDS and TB. God spoke to me and said 'After being treated like that, now you know how these other patients feel.' I learnt another lesson that day.

When the day came for my teeth to be removed, it turned out I knew the dentist as he treated the homeless guys at the Shelter I

---

[1] Heroin addicts often lose their teeth, due to lack of care and reliance on sugary foods/drinks whilst on the drug.

worked in. He said he had some bad news. Because I was still on interferon, I wasn't allowed any anaesthetic!

The beautiful thing is, the sister who had called me back before, had come in on her day off to be with me while it was done. So the dentist said 'How do you feel Bob?' I said 'I feel fine, because Jesus already told me this morning I'm not going to feel a thing!' I'd already prayed about it and felt God say I wouldn't feel it, til way after. So I had all eight teeth pulled out, on no anaesthetic, then I drove home... I felt it when I got home though! But it was fine, because God was with me and He sustained me.

The other good thing is, the hospital sorted out my teeth and did all my plates and dentures free of charge because of what had happened to me. So I learnt through all that, what it feels like to be a leper or an outcast. Even an experience that seemed so negative, God used for the good!

God also sends you people along the way to help you through these times. It was hard for the hospital to take my blood, as I had no useable veins left. But every time I went, a nurse called Mary looked after me and managed to get blood without turning me into a pin cushion. I know God sent her to look after me.

I have so many stories like this, I forget half of them! It makes you realise that life is this journey with God and nothing is wasted. He uses everything to help you understand and make you wiser. Almost straight away after this happened, an addict I knew from Glasgow turned up at the hostel I worked in. So I visited him in his flat in Shirley, and there were a load of other addicts shooting up in his room. I told him I couldn't talk to him there, but I'd wait in the hallway for him when he was finished.

That's when he said he'd had a letter the day before, confirming he had HIV AIDS. I had such compassion for him and I prayed with him there and then, outside his flat. I seemed to meet a lot of people with HIV AIDS after that. It's like God had prepared me, by giving me a glimpse of how they feel.

Redemption Story

'By His wounds, we are healed'
(Isaiah 53:5 NIV)

After a year, I was discharged from the liver clinic because they couldn't find a trace of Hepatitis C in my body. I had gone from having a year to live, to being completely healed by the power of Jesus! It's funny, even friends around me thought I was dying because of what the doctor said, but I never believed it. God had already taught me not to believe bad reports other human beings give me, but to trust what He has promised me. Who are you going to believe, man or God who created you? I've had no end of blood tests since and they still never find a trace of hepatitis in my body. Jesus healed me bit by bit over time and all I had to do was trust Him.

Another healing I received was in a place called Synagogue Church of all Nations, Nigeria. The first time I went to TB Joshua's church in Nigeria was in 2004. I had had 5 bleeds in my urine over the year and the doctors couldn't find out what was wrong with me. I was in a lot of pain in my back and I was on painkillers. When TB Joshua came to pray for me he said 'This is all connected to your past.' He didn't even touch me, but I fell on the floor and I had heat all over my body. I was on my knees, face down, and I couldn't get up because of the power of the Holy Spirit! Then after a bit he prayed again and said 'Father, disconnect him from the past!' Then all the pain left my body instantly.

For two years after that I had no back pain. But I was being silly and working too hard on the estate, carrying washing machines and stuff for other people. I knew I shouldn't be lifting, I just got stupid and really hurt my back again. The pain was awful – I knew I'd really damaged my back. I ended up on a lot of painkillers I really didn't want to be on. I said to God 'I know you love me and I know you're going to heal me.'

I returned to Nigeria where God totally healed me again! This time, I was walking through a tunnel in a place called Prayer Mountain. All of a sudden, a special song that God had given me that year when I was in so much pain, called 'Turning it around for me' by Vashawn Mitchell, started playing over the speakers. I couldn't believe it!

As I came out, TB Joshua was there and he said 'start praying.' So I dropped to my knees to pray and it felt like my back was on fire! The guys I was with couldn't even put their hands on my back there was that much heat coming off it! I was totally healed again. That's the real grace of God – He healed me twice of the same condition, even though I'd made such a mess of it all. He loves us to bits!

Throughout all this time, with my Hep C and back pain, I was still working on the Flowers' Estate. God showed me right at the beginning that my healing was tied up with the people on the Estate. Like I said before, Isaiah 58 talks about sharing food with the hungry and welcoming those who are outcast. But it then goes on to say our healing will 'break forth like the dawn.' I knew if I just carried on the work God had for me, He would heal me too. Whenever I've been away, as soon as I get back to the Flowers' Estate I know I am meant to be there. I feel like I belong there. It's the place where God has totally healed me.

If you or someone you know needs physical healing today, pray this prayer with me now:

Lord I thank you that you are the God of healing. I thank you that when Jesus died on the cross he took all our sickness and pain. I pray you would heal me today and make me new by the power of your blood. Amen.

Restoring Relationships

'I will restore to you the years that
the swarming locusts have eaten.'
(Joel 2:25 English Standard Version)

In my first marriage I was married for 16 years. When I got married in 1975, I was an addict and all that entailed, but I did get my act together when I returned to Southampton after not being allowed here for 3 years. I went to Sparsholt Agricultural College for one day a week to study Dairy Farming and I found I was really good at it. I even completed a City and Guilds qualification. The Principal at the College knew I was an addict, so he couldn't give me a reference, but he gave me a really good testimonial, which led to me getting a job on a farm in Dorset.

I looked after 98 cows and there was a cottage attached to the job, so I lived there with my wife and two children. I carried on using, and still had my prescription, even when I was working. My wife knew I was an addict. There were long periods of time though, where she thought I had stopped. But people were coming to visit me all the time, so it was a bit obvious.

From there we moved to Leicester, where I was contract milking and given 120 cows to look after. We lived in another cottage attached to the job and we were the only people living on the farm. I was milking cows three times a day at 4.30 am, 1pm and 9pm. It wasn't easy, as we had two small children by then and I was managing work, plus my addiction.

My kids did well though, as they were educated in village schools which were really small. It meant they were way ahead of other kids. They also got to live on different farms and enjoy different places. We spent some time in Wales, so my son was able to learn Welsh.

We moved about quite a bit with my job, every couple of years really. I was good at my job and I enjoyed it, but everywhere we went, people could see I was an addict. I'd be walking down the road in a new town and someone would come up to me and ask me if I wanted to score.[1]

The hours were long as well... Some nights I'd be out all night with the cows calving! It all got too much after a while. I still had my problems and when I was struggling with my drugs I used to drink as well. I'm not good with alcohol and would get into fights in the local pubs.

We ended up living in Nottingham and I was earning a decent wage, but overnight I lost 25% of my income, as we joined the Common Market. The Government introduced milk quotas, which meant the amount of milk we were allowed to produce dropped and the price of milk fell. This was a problem for me and my family as I was paid by the litre.

---

[1] Buy drugs

So I saw a job advertised in Davidstowe, Cornwall, looking after 280 cows. I went for the interview and got it straight away. It was a salary job, so I took it as I thought it would be more stable having an income for my kids. It wasn't a good move for me really, as there was a lot of drugs in Cornwall, which all seemed to find me overnight! Plus, other addicts I knew would come and visit me from Southampton, because I lived near the beach.

I wanted to get out of dairy farming, so I did a few other jobs after that. One was looking after a lady called Mrs Whitehouse. The deal was that we got to live on the top floor of a mansion, so long as we looked out for this elderly lady and took care of her sheep. The sheep were proper Cornish sheep, with long wool, that looked like Doogles.[2] They used to get wet in the rain and topple over. So one of my jobs was to pick the sheep up and put them back on their feet. I didn't realise then that I'd be doing the same thing years later, but with people!

Anyway, that family were kind to us and when Mrs. Whitehouse died, they helped me by writing a letter that got us to the top of the council house list. At that time there were hardly any council houses around, but we ended up in a brand new Housing Association house in a village called Splatt.

I was working three or four jobs at that time and I was still caught up in all the drugs. Some friends and I were growing masses of cannabis too. I was getting pulled right back into it all. I used to just keep myself to myself and didn't talk about it with my wife. I'd get stuff in the post from Southampton, but would keep it

---

[2] A character on the kids' TV show 'The Magic Roundabout'

secret. A lot of the time, I think she thought I was drug free when really I wasn't.

Then, when my kids were older, my wife started working for Social Services. We grew apart, as I didn't fit in with it all because of my lifestyle. From there, for about four years, I stayed in the house but slept on the sofa. My wife blamed it on all my jobs, so she wanted me to find a proper job with one salary.

I sent a cheeky letter to the local cheese factory. I wrote 'I've gone to a lot of trouble to write this letter, so please don't put it in the bin!' The manager liked my cheek, so he phoned me up and offered me a job. I was on quite a big prescription for my drugs at the time, but the factory knew and they let me go and pick up my script every morning. They liked me there because I could do two eight hour shifts in a row, then sit up and watch telly all night. I was on a lot of Speed[3] at the time too!

I was a skeleton by this time. I remember one of my neighbours saying to my wife 'Can't you see your husband is disappearing before your eyes?' I knew I had to leave. It was getting worse and it wasn't doing me or my family any good.

I love my kids and it broke me leaving them. I'd never been separated from them until then. Even when they were little we never had babysitters, they were always with me. So I packed up my car one day and just left. I felt like I was dying and I needed to leave for the sake of everyone.

---

[3] Methamphetamine used to keep people energised/alert

This was my rock bottom. I have never felt so broken hearted in my life. I couldn't cope with it. I'd never been away from my children and it broke me inside. I remember standing on a beach in Bude in the middle of the night - I had just reached the end of myself. I had enough drugs on me to do myself in.

I screamed to the stars, 'If you can't take this feeling away from me, I'm out of here now!' That's when I knew there was a God. I didn't know what to call him or anything, but this total peace just came over me.

The day after this, I told some Christian traveller friends, Holga and Vi, what had happened. They said 'you've gotta come to church, Bob.' So that evening they took me to Dowinney Mission, this little green shed in the middle of nowhere.

David Chaudry was preaching that night and it was like everything he was saying was just for me. He said 'So, who wants to give their lives to Jesus?' And I stood up – I was the only one, but I knew I had to do it. Ken and Hilda were with me that night too and I was even baptised a few weeks later.

The problem is, I was still a mess. My life was chaos. I was so far gone on drugs and my mind was under attack from all these voices. I was doing more drugs than ever before! It wasn't until about 12 months later (when Barry invited me to live in his caravan) that things really started changing for me.

That's why I never give up on addicts – even if they have become Christians and been baptised. With Jesus, it's a process and I believe He can set anyone free from addiction. With me, it took a year, but it could take longer! It's all in His time and he wants to use us to see other people freed. If it wasn't for Ken and Hilda's love, and their prayers that day, I wouldn't be here now.

God never gave up on me, so I don't give up on anyone. God showed me later that He can't resist a contrite heart.[4] I knew I had messed up my whole life and I was humble. And even in my worst state as a Christian, God was speaking to me.

I remember waking up one morning with a daft story about a pearl in my head. It was about a man who sold everything he had, to own this pearl. I couldn't understand why someone would give everything up for something so small. Then Ken showed me it was a story in the Bible that Jesus had told. It was all about how we have to let everything go, so we can have the prize – Jesus!

Christians have always played a big part in my life, even when I didn't know it. I remember turning up at this pastor's house at 2am one morning, after doing enough drugs to kill me. He grabbed my hand and cried out 'Jesus, save this man's life!' His name was Richard Uglow. He was a good man.

Another time, I didn't have any tax on my car and this Christian guy Jules said he'd been praying that morning and God told him to give me his book full of car tax stamps. There was enough to pay for the year… And this was all while I was on my way to pick up my prescription!

---

[4] Psalm 51

I destroyed my marriage with my first wife, through the use of drugs and I wrecked my relationship with my two children. For that I am really sorry. I trust that one day Jesus will restore my relationship with my children in the same way he has restored the rest of my life. I don't blame anyone for what happened or hold it against anyone. It was my addiction and that had never really been dealt with. But it's been dealt with now, through Jesus, and I am a completely different person!

You see, God is pursuing you, even when you don't realise it. Even when you're messed up on drugs and all your relationships have failed, he is still watching over you and waiting for you to come to Him.

Redemption Story

Then the LORD God said,
'It is not good for the man to be alone.
I will make a partner who is just right for him.'
(Genesis 2:18)

I'd been a drug free Christian for about a year. I was doing odd jobs for people in the church, driving tractors and milking cows. I used to milk at four in the morning, get home for eight, have a shower then go out and work for Jesus! I'd drive down to Plymouth and different places, to share my testimony with people and pray for those who had similar stories to mine. It was amazing! I saw people coming off drugs, just like me. That was my new life and I loved it.

My prayer every day to God, was to send me a wife because I didn't want to be on my own for the rest of my life. I was willing to stay single if He'd wanted me to, but I used to find it hard on Sundays after church, when other people went home with their families and I was alone. That's why it's so important to welcome single people into our families!

Ken and Hilda were good to me and made me a part of their family and I wasn't really looking around, but I knew God wanted to give me a partner. I trusted God totally, that He would give me the perfect person for what He wanted me to do.

Anyway, two friends of mine Holga and Vi, who had also come off drugs and become Christians, were having a party. They were an amazing couple! They were the ones who had invited me to church for the first time and they even let me live with them for a bit when I was still injecting myself.

I remember it was Vi's birthday and I'd just got back from Plymouth where I'd seen God do amazing things. I'd stopped at the garage to buy her some flowers and I was just gonna pop in to wish her a happy birthday and that. I wasn't planning to stay long.

When I walked in the door, I looked across the room and I saw Colette. The Holy Spirit spoke to me and said 'This is the woman you are going to marry.' To which my response was 'Well I hope you've told her that!' So I got chatting to her and we really hit it off. I didn't tell her what God had said 'til after we got married, as I didn't want to pressure her. But I knew it was right. Colette was staying with Vi and Holga for a bit, along with her little girl Zoë who was aged two and a half at the time. So I started going round every day for Bible study with them all.

It wasn't straight forward, as Colette had escaped an abusive marriage and her husband had disappeared to Australia on a bender.[5] I got a bit of a hard time from the church for spending time with her, as she was still technically married to the guy. I think they were trying to protect me really. But I knew what God had said, so I didn't worry about it too much. I had already decided I was going to obey God, not man.

Colette lived in Malmsbury, so I got a job up there roofing and working for agencies, but it just wasn't working out money wise. I was overqualified for a lot of the farming jobs there and the money wasn't enough. I knew God had closed the door on me. It pushed me back to Southampton, where I moved back in with my mum. So I lived in Southampton and visited Col on the weekends.

From there, God told me to find a church. So I used to walk from the Flower Roads, right into town every Sunday to attend Community Church. He told me I wasn't always gonna like it, but that was where He wanted me to be. Any rate, me and my friend Walati used to walk together and we'd always meet a non-believer on the street and take him with us!

I joined a Church Home Group on Stoneham Lane with a couple called Fred and Trish. It was just us and one other guy. When

---

[5] Alcohol and drugs binge

Fred asked what he thought we should do, I told him in Cornwall we used to do a lot of prayer walking,[6] to open up areas to Jesus. He said 'That's funny, because God told me to do that months ago and I haven't done it!' So that's what we started doing. I look at it now and every road we prayed on, there are now Christians living on it. There weren't any when we started all those years ago!

Then one day, we were praying on Bluebell Road and God started really talking to me from Isaiah 61, that there would be Oaks of Righteousness[7] in every street on the Flower Roads. He said to me 'You told me you would go anywhere for me, well I'm asking you to come back here.' So I had no choice! I was back where I had started taking drugs, but this time it was different.

That night I rang Colette up. She'd been on the Council list for three years and she'd been offered that same day, a cottage in a pretty little village near Malmsbury. She'd even been given the key! We'd been talking about getting married and that, so I said 'I've just said yes to God for coming back to Southampton, so if you take the cottage you'll have to live there on your own.' She said I better come up that weekend so we could talk!

Four days later, I was up visiting her and we went to Swindon Community Church. The preacher hadn't turned up, so a couple stood at the front and shared about how God had got them living

---

[6] Walking streets and praying for a particular area

[7] They will be called oaks of righteousness, a planting of the Lord for the display of his splendour. (Isaiah 61:3)

on a council estate. Then, we were talking to the family sitting in front of us and I ended up telling them what God had said to me about moving back to the Flowers' Estate. It turned out they were from Southampton. The woman said 'Oh, I know a couple with a house on Laburnum Road. I'll give you their number.'

We went there to look at it and I knew it was the right thing. I didn't have any money for a deposit at the time, but God woke the landlord in the night and told them to drop the rent right down and waive the deposit. God had opened a door that no one could close!

We got married in September 1996 but had to wait before we moved into our house, as there was a tenant already living there. So we moved into a place in Midanbury, up on the hill overlooking Southampton. This was the time when God started to prepare us for what was to come and told us to start praying together.

During those 6 months or so, God spoke to us clearly. It was difficult for Colette, and she didn't quite get it until God woke her up one night and spoke to her about the Harvest being ready. He said there were souls on the estate, he wanted her to win for Jesus. So we started our journey together. I could never have done it without her!

It's so good to be with Colette. For me, she is the most real Christian I have ever met. She's a Holy Spirit lady! God speaks to us both about the same things, all the time. We work well together, even through the difficult times. God's taught me so much being with her that I never knew in my first marriage. We keep short accounts with each other and as head of the household, the Holy Spirit often gets me to apologise for things first! We're honest with each other too, which is something I didn't have before. Jesus has given me my perfect partner and restored my life completely.

With Zoë too, it's been a beautiful journey. I considered her my own daughter from day one. I actually tried to adopt her when she was little, but Social Services couldn't track down Colette's ex to get his permission. So she waited 'til she was 16, then changed her surname to Light! I am so proud of her and the woman she has become. She's such a well-balanced person who gets on with everyone, no matter what background they are from. She doesn't judge anyone.

We've had 18 years living on Laburnum Road, with no privacy and the door knocking day and night. We've seen God move and we've seen miracles. We've seen the Holy Spirit changing people's lives right in front of us. We've baptised loads of people together. And all this just because we said yes to Jesus when He asked us to live on the estate. It's simple really! He's just taught us to love people the way He does... And He gives us that love in the first place. Jesus is incredible!

This is my life.

This is My Offering to Him!

Acknowledgements

F irstly, I would like to thank all those who have helped me in my life; the many friends who have inspired me and challenged me along the way. I want to say a special thank you to my wife Colette, without whom I would not be where I am today. Also, my three children Zoë, Jessica, and Sam, whom I love dearly.

I'd like to thank my best friends Gary and Teri Stache for always supporting us and believing God's vision for our community. Their generosity is truly incredible. I am deeply grateful for my pastors in Cornwall, Ken and Hilda, to whom I owe so much. The love they showed me through Jesus, saved my life!

There are so many more, without whom this book would not have been written: Marion Lloyd, Dave Danson, Suzanne Baker, Fred Gardener; I am grateful you are in my life and your continued support is deeply appreciated. I'd also like to thank Sarah Little and the Sedbed Trust for helping me to actually write this book.

Thank you to all those who live and serve on the Flowers' Estate and I have the privilege of working alongside, I thank you from the bottom of my heart. You are a treasure in God's kingdom!

But finally, the biggest thank you of all has to go to Jesus, the one who saved me from myself. The one who's name is above all names. Thank you for giving me the gift of having you in my life!

If you would like to find out more about Bob's work,
or get in touch with him, please visit
www.flowerofjustice.com

If this book has impacted you or you have said any of the prayers, I encourage you to find some Christians who will chat with you and pray. If you don't know any, you can find a list of your local churches at www.findachurch.co.uk

To obtain more copies of this book
or to contact Bob in person,
please email lightbob51@aol.com